negotiating
persuading and
influencing

ALAN FOWLER

Alan Fowler has worked widely in both the private and public sectors, with personnel appointments in four industries and two local authorities. He is now a freelance consultant, a director of Personnel Publications Ltd, and a member of the editorial board of *People Management*, the bimonthly journal of the IPD. He writes widely on personnel issues, with regular articles in *People Management* and the *Local Government Chronicle*. His books include (in the *Management Shapers* series) *The Disciplinary Interview* (1996) and *Writing Job Descriptions* (1997); and *Get More – and More Value – from Your People* (1998) and *Get More – and More Results – from Your People* (1998) – all published by the IPD.

Management Shapers is a comprehensive series covering all the crucial management skill areas. Each book includes the key issues, helpful starting points and practical advice in a concise and lively style. Together, they form an accessible library reflecting current best practice – ideal for study or quick reference.

Other titles in the series:

The Appraisal Discussion
Terry Gillen

Constructive Feedback
Roland and Frances Bee

The Disciplinary Interview
Alan Fowler

Listening Skills (second edition)
Ian MacKay

The Selection Interview
Penny Hackett

The Institute of Personnel and Development is the leading publisher of books and reports for personnel and training professionals, students, and all those concerned with the effective management and development of people at work. For full details of all our titles please contact the Publishing Department:

tel. 0181-263 3387
fax 0181-263 3850
e-mail publish@ipd.co.uk
The catalogue of all IPD titles can be viewed on the IPD website:
http://www.ipd.co.uk

negotiating
persuading and
influencing

ALAN FOWLER

INSTITUTE OF PERSONNEL AND DEVELOPMENT

First published in the *Training Extras* series in 1995

Reprinted 1997

First published in the *Management Shapers* series in 1998

Typesetting by Paperweight
Printed in Great Britain by
The Guernsey Press, Channel Islands

British Library Cataloguing in Publication Data
A catalogue record for this book is available from the British Library

ISBN
0-85292-755-X

**INSTITUTE OF PERSONNEL
AND DEVELOPMENT**

IPD House, Camp Road, London SW19 4UX
Tel.: 0181 971 9000   Fax: 0181 263 3333
Registered office as above. Registered Charity No. 1038333.
A company limited by guarantee. Registered in England No. 2931892.

contents

all managers negotiate

The nature of negotiation

Most managers spend much of their working time in contact with colleagues and other persons over whom they have no executive authority. Some studies have shown that as little as 10 per cent of managers' time may be spent with the employees who report directly to them. Part of the balance is spent alone – reading the mail or planning work programmes, for example – but much of the day is occupied with discussions and meetings with other managers, or with suppliers or customers.

In these contacts, in which results cannot be achieved simply by issuing instructions, progress is made by discussion, argument and agreement. You approach a colleague for information that you need for a report. They respond initially by saying they are too busy to provide it, so you try to persuade them to change their mind. A colleague contacts you to ask if you can transfer one of your staff to them for a short period to help with an urgent project. You are reluctant because of your own work priorities, but are prepared to talk about alternative ways in which you might help. The discussions involved in situations of this kind are, in essence, negotiations.

Even within an executive relationship, situations often arise in which persuasion is more effective than instruction. You may ask (not tell) one of your staff to take on a particular project. They may initially be reluctant to agree, so a discussion ensues in which you try to convince them of the good reasons for your request. Or you may approach your line boss with a suggestion or request that they have the authority to reject; but they are willing, instead, to be convinced by the case you make. These types of discussion are also forms of negotiation.

Negotiation occurs whenever there is an issue that cannot be resolved by one person acting alone; it occurs when the two (or more) people who have to be involved begin with different views on how to proceed, or have different aims for the outcome. There are two situations in which negotiation does not, or cannot, occur:

● when one of the two persons immediately agrees to what the other is asking or suggesting

■ when one of the two adamantly refuses even to discuss the matter.

The same principles apply to both formal and informal situations. If your colleague simply agrees to your request for information, no negotiation is necessary. If, in a commercial situation, a supplier simply refuses to discuss a price reduction, no negotiation is possible. But in very many situations there is neither immediate acceptance nor refusal, and the two persons begin to talk with a view to reaching an agreed conclusion.

Influence and persuasion

The outcome of such a discussion will be affected in part by the facts of the issue being addressed. But negotiations are very rarely concluded simply on the basis of a wholly objective, logical and factual analysis. Two major and more subjective factors are involved – *influence* and *persuasion*.

Influence is a broad concept, involving the effect on each person of the whole context in which the discussion takes place, including the quality of past and present working relationships, as well as each participant's unspoken ambitions or fears. Persuasion involves all those skills of argument and discussion that can be used by one person to obtain another's agreement. Understanding and using influence purposefully, and developing persuasive skills, are important components in the toolkit of the effective manager. Recognising when and how these skills are being used on you by your colleagues and others is of similar importance.

Three provisos

Before looking at influence and persuasion in detail, there are three provisos to consider:

1. Managers sometimes negotiate when they do not need to. If you have the authority to make a decision, it is

probably unwise to behave as though nothing can be done unless other people are persuaded to agree. It is however good management practice to explain your decisions and to make them after obtaining other people's views. There are also situations in which, although you have the authority to make a unilateral decision, you decide *not* to exercise the right to decide and instead, to gain commitment, use persuasion and influence to obtain agreement (which may involve compromise). But there are, equally, situations in which your managerial authority will be weakened if you give the impression that something you have the authority to decide is open to a negotiated compromise. A useful general guideline is: *don't negotiate when you don't need to, unless there are good reasons.*

2. Following this guideline while avoiding acting autocratically requires a clear distinction between negotiation and consultation. There is a crucial difference between asking people to agree and asking them for their views. Negotiation implies that both persons accept that agreement between them is needed before a decision can be implemented. Consultation implies a willingness by one person to listen and respond to the views of others, while reserving the right to make the final decision. The guideline is: *always make clear whether you are seeking agreement or inviting comment.*

3. There may be occasions when, after some discussion, it becomes clear that you or the other person must hold a

position without alteration or compromise. What happens then is either that one party concedes, or an impasse is reached. If deadlock is clearly inevitable there is no point in wasting time on further argument or recrimination which may well exacerbate relationships. Some other form of resolution will be needed – such as referring the matter to a senior manager or seeking advice from other colleagues. In a formal setting this amounts to the use of conciliation or arbitration. Informally it can be just an agreement to disagree and to seek assistance from others in resolving the matter. *If deadlock occurs, try to obtain agreement to seeking help from others.*

How often do you negotiate?

Keep detailed work time sheets for a week and then complete the questionnaire on page 6. 'Negotiation' is any form of meeting or discussion in which you and/or the persons you are in contact with use argument and persuasion to achieve an agreed decision or action.

Activity	Approx. % of time	Negotiation involved	
		Yes	No
Working alone			
Contact with:			
own staff: informal			
formal (meetings etc)			
own boss: informal			
formal			
colleagues: informal			
formal			
suppliers, customers etc:			
formal			
informal			
Other activities (travelling etc)			

Total % of time spent in activities in which negotiation occurs ...... %

2 influence

The importance of influence

The outcome of a negotiation is rarely determined simply by the facts of the matter or even the persuasive skills of those concerned. Other factors are usually involved, even if these are unstated or unrecognised. Consider any recent experience you have had, either of trying to persuade a colleague to agree to something you want, or of being subject yourself to an attempt at persuasion by someone else, and then answer the questions in the table on page 8.

These questions are not comprehensive. There are many factors that can influence how a discussion proceeds and affect its conclusion. Recognising and making use of these factors can be extremely helpful, both in creating a context in which your persuasive skills will be more effective, and in preventing you from being unduly influenced by things not directly relevant to the matter in hand. This range of influences can be categorised under a number of headings:

- personal relationships – short- and long-term

- status differences

- ▲ connections with sources of organisational power

	Yes	No

- ○ Did you find in yourself (or detect in the other person) any tendency to be influenced by considerations other than the details of the topic under discussion?
- ▣ Did you feel confident?
- △ If yes, was this because you were more experienced than the other person?
- ○ If no, was this because you thought the other person carried more organisational 'clout'?
- ○ Were you up against time pressures?
- ○ Were you concerned about your reputation if you failed in your objective?

- ● formality
- ● information and expertise
- ● gender, race and age differences
- ▣ reputation – for success or failure
- ▲ expectations about outcomes
- ● timing – durations and deadlines
- ● work pressures
- ● location – the negotiating environment.

Personal relationships

How vigorously or tactfully someone argues their case is often influenced by two considerations about the quality of their personal working relationship with the other person:

● Has there been a past history of a friendly, collaborative relationship, or have previous working contacts been coloured by unhelpful or antagonistic attitudes?

■ Might the way the current negotiation develops improve or damage future working relationships?

These considerations are often of greater influence in informal discussions between colleagues than in formal negotiations with external contacts. For example, there will be no past history to influence negotiations with a potential new supplier, and if these negotiations break down, then the immediate relationship is dissolved with no ongoing effects. On the other hand, an unpleasant disagreement with a colleague – even over a relatively minor matter – may be the last straw in a deteriorating history of bad feeling; or may upset what had until then been a sound working relationship.

Linked to the influence of specific episodes in previous working contacts is the simple factor of personal likes and dislikes. If you like the other person, you may be too ready to concede points that should be resisted. If you dislike them, you risk treating everything they say as negative and succumbing to a temptation to score points rather than resolve the issue under discussion. Neither person in such situations may actually refer to this personal relationship factor, though both may be strongly influenced by it. You need to be honest with yourself about this. Ask yourself: *Am I likely to be either unduly belligerent or unnecessarily compliant in this discussion because of the way I feel about the other person?*

Concern about future working relationships is in some circumstances a legitimate factor to consider. The matter under discussion may in itself be of minor importance, though you perhaps know that it is a potentially sensitive issue with your colleague. So it may not be worth the risk of damaging what has been a collaborative relationship by pressing this one issue too hard. Alternatively you may need to consider whether a quick concession on an issue being urged on you by a colleague could contribute to an undesirable reputation for being easily persuaded. These are matters of judgement for which no general rule can be suggested, other than to ask yourself: *Should my position on this issue take into account the possible effect on future working relationships?*

Finally, there is the question of mutual obligations. Your colleague asks you to help out with a work problem 'as a favour', perhaps with a reminder that he or she has previously helped you in a similar situation. The more subtle approach may not include any mention of past events, but the way the request is put carries the implication that a return favour is owed. Some managers are very manipulative in this respect, offering help or support from time to time in order to create a sense of obligation that they can later exploit to their advantage.

While there may be occasions when the expectation of a return favour is justified, there is a considerable risk that a sense of obligation will distort or weaken the position that ought to be taken on the issue under discussion. Negotiation on the basis of trading favours cannot be recommended as a satisfactory strategy. Being aware of the potential influence of this factor goes a long way towards preventing its adverse effect. So ask yourself: *Am I being unduly influenced by a sense of obligation? Am I expecting to achieve too much by trying to exploit a sense of obligation?*

Status differences

A manager in one part of an organisation who is trying to obtain agreement to some course of action from a senior manager in another part may well feel inhibited by formal status differences. The two may be equally involved in the issue under discussion and the senior manager may in fact have no authority to give instructions to the other manager – who is not one of his or her staff. Nevertheless, both may be conscious of their differences of formal status, and this is likely to affect how each behaves in the ensuing discussion. The advantage (in terms of influence) lies with the senior of the two, unless the junior manager can set aside any feelings of inferiority and retain confidence on the grounds of their legitimate involvement in the issue concerned and their knowledge of the subject matter.

Some senior managers exploit this factor, using two different approaches:

● They may treat less senior staff from other sections in an abrupt, unhelpful and overtly status-conscious manner in order to undermine confidence and so weaken the other person's ability to present a persuasive case.

■ They may project an unusually friendly attitude, designed to make the less senior person feel relieved that rank is not being pulled, and therefore reluctant to press points that might upset the unexpectedly pleasant senior. In reality, this false friendliness is both patronising and manipulative.

When negotiating occurs between boss and subordinate (ie about an issue on which the boss has chosen not to exercise decision-making authority), it is almost inevitable that some status considerations will apply. If you are the boss, you will probably feel that if the matter cannot be agreed, you can impose a decision. If you are the subordinate, you will be aware of this and may also stop short of voicing some concerns or criticisms because you do not want to damage the relationship with your boss. There are lessons here for both parties:

- If you are the boss, make clear at the outset whether you are genuinely willing to abide by the agreed outcome of the discussion or whether, in reality, the matter is one for consultation rather than negotiation.

- If you are the subordinate, and you have a good case, do not be inhibited because the other person is your boss: this may influence how you present your case but it should not influence its content.

For a senior manager or boss there are several potential disadvantages in using status differences to influence negotiation. If you rebuff a less senior person from another part of the organisation the result may simply be that you are then approached by that person's manager, on whom status influence will not be effective. Using status influence may prevent you hearing things you ought to know from subordinates who have become reluctant to speak out.

Connection with sources of organisational power

This factor is somewhat similar to status influence, though it is often more subtle or indirect. A crude illustration of this factor is when the person you are dealing with may be relatively junior but is known to have an unusually close working (or personal) relationship with an influential senior manager. You may therefore be wary of what you say, in case adverse comments about you are relayed to this manager. Whether such considerations should influence you is a matter of judgement. Ideally, these situations would not occur, but in many organisations an understanding of what amounts to organisational politics may, from a pragmatic viewpoint, be desirable.

In a reverse situation, your confidence in negotiating with a manager in another part of the organisation may be boosted by knowing that you have backing for your position from your own boss, or from the whole of your management team. A more impersonal aspect, which has the same effect, is the knowledge that the position you are taking can be shown to be consistent with the organisation's core values, business plan or mission statement.

In most organisations, the real centres or sources of power (and therefore influence) are not precisely those implied by the formal organisation chart. Some managers will be known to be listened to by the chief executive more than others; or there may be a specialist, or perhaps an 'elder statesman', who although not at the top of the hierarchy is respected by everyone for the wisdom of their opinions or the quality of their expertise. Your negotiating position will consequently be strengthened if you know you have their support for whatever it is you are trying to achieve.

This type of influence needs to be handled sensitively. Simply to state that a particular viewpoint ought to be accepted because it accords with the views of someone influential may well generate resentment. On the other hand, if the connection is not recognised, it can have no direct effect (other than to boost the confidence of the person putting the view forward). It may therefore be appropriate to introduce the matter into the discussion – though more as a helpful hint than a threat. Say something like: 'Incidentally, I happened to be talking to George about this the other day and he seemed to agree with the point I'm making.' Don't say: 'If you don't agree I will have to see George about it, because he has already told me I'm right!' The general points to consider are these:

● Check whether the attitude of the person you are trying to persuade is likely to be affected by their connections with any sources of power within the organisation.

▪ Check whether your position would be strengthened by having the support of other influential people in the organisation, and/or by being shown to be consistent with the organisation's aims, values and business plans.

Formality

Some managers who are very competent in one-to-one, informal discussions lose this confidence if they have to conduct a formal negotiation. They are inhibited by the fact that the meeting has been described specifically as a negotiation (eg to negotiate a revised rental for an office building, or a new price for a contract). This is probably because they have not recognised what they do in informal discussions as negotiation, and therefore have little feel for how the skills they exercise in those discussions are transferable to a formal setting.

Yet as the first section of this book makes clear, an informal meeting in which two managers with different viewpoints seek by discussion to persuade each other to change – though with a view to reaching a mutually satisfactory outcome – involves the very essence of negotiation. So the first point is: *remember that persuasive skills used in informal situations are transferable to formal negotiations.*

There are two main differences between informal and formal negotiations:

● In formal negotiations the discussion is more structured, and the various negotiating stages described later in this book are more clearly defined.

■ Many formal negotiations are between teams, rather than just two individuals.

To some extent, both these factors can make formal negotiations easier to handle than informal ones, in which it may be far from clear what each person's objectives really are, and for which no preparation has been made.

For example, a colleague may drop in to your office and say, 'Have you got a few minutes to talk about a problem I've got on my plate?' You agree, thinking he or she simply wants your comment or advice. However, after a while, it becomes evident that they are really wanting you to take or support some specific action that you have not had time to consider and are not particularly happy about. But by the time you realise this, you may already have unwittingly committed yourself to comments that make it difficult for you to draw back. In a formal negotiation, the subject matter will normally have been defined and agreed before the meeting, so there is no ambiguity of purpose and there will have been time to prepare.

In a team negotiation, this preparation can include deciding what role each team member will play. For a team of three, a very effective arrangement is:

● One person leads with a constructive, problem-solving approach.

■ Another person adopts a more critical, questioning stance, probing for weaknesses in the other team's case.

▲ The third person plays a more observational role, keeping notes, but also acting as a 'sweeper' to bring in any points missed by the other two.

In informal, one-to-one discussions, all these roles have to be played by one person. There is no real reason, therefore, to be inhibited by formality. Instead: *use formality to obtain the advantages of clarity of subject and purpose, preparation time, and (in a team situation) a useful distribution of roles.*

Information and expertise

In most negotiations, formal or informal, the person who knows most about the subject under discussion has an influential advantage. This is partly a matter of personal confidence. If you are dealing with a topic in which you know that you have had more experience or that you have studied more extensively than the other person you should have fewer worries about being ambushed by some unexpected argument, and feel confident that you can quote all the necessary facts to support your case. This know-how factor can be particularly important for anyone inhibited by personality factors or status. These inhibitions can be largely offset by the confidence that derives from a high level of expertise about the relevant subject matter.

To gain full advantage, however, you have to make the other person recognise this difference in know-how – you gain nothing by hiding your light under a bushel. This may involve several measures:

● It may be possible to support what you are saying with a handout setting out statistics or other material that demonstrate your grasp of the subject.

■ You may be able to use a flipchart to highlight key points and make plain the flow of your argument.

▲ You must be prepared to be assertive – in a pleasant and positive way – and inject into the discussion all the relevant information of which you, but perhaps not the other person, have knowledge.

There may be occasions when it is the other person, not you, who is evidently the more knowledgeable. This is uncomfortable, and there are three possible responses:

● You may try to defer further discussion so that you can find out more about the subject yourself.

■ You may seek the assistance of another expert in the subject and perhaps take him or her with you to the discussion.

▲ You need to be very clear whether expertise on points of detail is truly important in deciding the issue under discussion. It may be that the other person will try to 'blind you with science', spouting facts that on close examination are not really relevant.

The principal points to remember are:

● Check who is the better informed about the subject under discussion: you or the other person.

■ If it is you, use this to boost your confidence, but also make sure the other person recognises your expertise.

▲ If it is the other person, either improve your own knowledge or seek support from someone as knowledgeable as the other person.

Gender, race and age differences

The inhibiting influence of differences of gender, race or age between the two persons in a negotiation is similar in its effect to differences of status. One person will act in a superior manner, the other may consequently feel at a disadvantage and their confidence or ability to press their view will be undermined.

Both gender and age can be factors in the way some men behave in a discussion with significantly younger women. This behaviour can range from the dismissive or downright rude to the irritatingly patronising or the offensively frivolous. These extremes may be met only occasionally, and if they involve race or gender may need to be dealt with as a discrimination problem, separate from any specific negotiating incident. It is more common for *tendencies* towards these types of behaviour to occur; these are largely unconscious and may not be intended to irritate or cause concern. There are two ways of dealing with them:

● to terminate the discussion, saying it is not possible to continue unless the other person is prepared to take the matter seriously and sensibly

■ to keep any (understandable) emotional reaction under control, concentrate on the issue under discussion, and continue to put your own case firmly and confidently.

Occasionally you may experience (or perhaps be guilty of) a reverse form of behaviour, in which a young, enthusiastic manager displays an unacceptable lack of patience or respect for a much older colleague. The resentment this may cause will have the opposite impact to the aim of all effective negotiation – which is to achieve a mutually satisfactory agreement. If you, as the older person, experience this behaviour it may be necessary to stop the discussion, making it clear you are not prepared to continue until the younger person is ready to listen to your views. If you, as the younger person, find yourself behaving in this way towards someone older remember that experience may have taught them to be more cautious than you, and that you are extremely unlikely to win the argument if you antagonise them.

● Check whether you are being adversely influenced, or are exerting adverse influence, because of differences of race, gender or age.

▣ If you are affected, make a positive decision either to stop the discussion and tackle the unacceptable behaviour head on; or just to keep cool, ignore any provocation, and press on with your case.

▲ If you find yourself exerting this type of influence, stop it – not only because it is offensive in itself, but also because it distorts attention from the issue under discussion.

Reputation

Both people in a negotiation may be deeply concerned about how the outcome will affect their reputation with colleagues or bosses. They may look forward to announcing they have won an important concession from their 'opponent'; or fear criticism if they are perceived to have failed, or conceded too much. This emphasis on 'winning' or 'losing' leads to a confrontational approach which may damage working relationships, or to such unwillingness to consider any form of compromise that the negotiation simply breaks down.

One trap to avoid is telling colleagues about a forthcoming discussion in overoptimistic terms eg 'I've got a meeting with Jill this afternoon about changing the date for the monthly cost analysis, and I'm really going to take her apart!' Jill may, however, produce unexpectedly good reasons why she cannot do what you want. How do you then describe the outcome to your colleagues?

The reputation to aim for is not one for winning a given argument but for skill in solving problems and developing effective working relationships. This will not be achieved by overconcern about how any single negotiation may be perceived by other people. Boasting about successes may also store up future difficulties, because it may tempt some colleagues to look for later opportunities to turn the tables. Being oversensitive about a reputation for compromise or for making concessions will undermine your self-confidence and encourage a brittle, rather than flexible, negotiating style.

If you perceive the other person in a negotiation to be highly influenced by these considerations of reputation, you will need to help them see the advantages to them of any concession they may make (a point developed in more detail in Chapter 3). You will also need to avoid any implication that you enjoy 'beating' them, or that you will relay the outcome of the discussion to your colleagues in terms of winning or losing. Sensitivity to the other person's motivation and self-esteem is an essential element of effective negotiation. *Aim to achieve a reputation for solving problems, not for winning or losing.*

Expectations about outcomes

Inexperienced negotiators are often unduly influenced by unrealistic expectations about the likely outcome. They are convinced their view of the matter is correct and that the logic of the arguments they are planning to use is overwhelming. They then run into two difficulties. First, the other person produces facts they have not previously thought about; and second, arguments based simply on logic turn out to be far less persuasive than expected. Because of unpreparedness for these difficulties, the inexperienced lose confidence and may themselves be persuaded to agree to less than satisfactory outcomes.

This factor may be exacerbated if bosses or colleagues reinforce the unrealistic expectations – either through overoptimism or by thinking misguidedly that the negotiators' confidence can be boosted by saying how strong their case is eg 'Don't worry: you've got an indisputable case and we don't see how you can possibly lose!'

Sometimes the reverse occurs. The negotiator may have too limited or pessimistic an expectation and go into the discussion with already weakened confidence and resolve. The cause may be one or other of the factors considered earlier, such as feelings of inferiority or worries about the adequacy of know-how.

Either way, there are often two underlying flaws:

● The issue has not been considered from the other person's viewpoint. When you are preparing for a negotiation it pays to play devil's advocate (or ask a colleague to do this) and look for weaknesses in your own case and for strengths in the other party's.

■ Too specific or detailed a view is taken of the probable outcome, with insufficient attention being given to a range of solutions or to the need to be flexible and ingenious during the discussion.

In discussing the issue with your boss or colleagues before the negotiation it is far better to emphasise potential difficulties than to give assurances about outcomes you may not be able to deliver. The old marketing maxim 'Underpromise, overperform' should be kept in mind. *Ensure your expectations, and those of your boss and colleagues, are realistic – ie based on a thorough assessment of the strengths and weaknesses of both your own case and the likely case of your 'opponent'.*

Timing

Two aspects of time can powerfully influence how a negotiation is handled, and therefore its outcome:

● *duration* – the amount of time available for discussion

■ *deadlines* – the importance of an outcome being determined by a specified date.

To give an example: you are to meet with a colleague to resolve a difference of view between your section and theirs about the design of a new customer complaints procedure. They agree a date for the meeting but say, 'We're extremely busy at the moment – it shouldn't take more than hour, should it?', going on to suggest sandwiching the meeting between two others they have already scheduled. Do you agree, or do you say that because the issue is very important, quite complicated, and should not be rushed, an hour is inadequate?

Obviously no general rule can be suggested – though questions of this kind are important. You will therefore need to consider several factors:

● From your knowledge of the issue, the probable position to be taken by your colleague and their general decision-making style or personality, are you most likely to obtain a good outcome by a brisk, no-nonsense meeting? Or is it likely that a careful, longer and more exploratory discussion would be more effective?

● If you agree to a short meeting, but this fails to resolve the matter, will it be satisfactory simply to adjourn and resume on another occasion? Or would this break in discussion give the other person time to think of more points with which to counter your case?

■ Which is your preferred mode or style of negotiation with regard to time – an open-ended approach to allow for very thorough discussion, or a time-limited approach to encourage concentration on key points?

In general, there is a tendency to underestimate how long it takes to discuss and resolve an issue on which two people initially have different views. The reason is that achieving agreement requires people to accept the reality of views different from their own and to accept change or compromise. It is not just a matter of putting forward a set of facts and expecting the other person immediately to accept the logic of the exposition. They (and probably you) have to be persuaded and helped to feel comfortable about the outcome that is eventually agreed. People need time to make this adjustment in attitude and react badly to any attempt to rush them into an agreement.

There are, however, a few tactical approaches that can help

to prevent an unproductively lengthy discussion:

● If it is thought two hours should be adequate, the meeting can be timed to start mid-morning or mid-afternoon. The imminent arrival of the normal lunch time or evening office closure may then provide a useful and impersonal stimulus to bring the discussion to a satisfactory conclusion.

■ It may sometimes be better to use the telephone rather than a face-to-face discussion. Research indicates that on relatively simple issues telephone discussions may be both quicker and more effective. Matters can sometimes be resolved with a 10-minute phone conversation that would take at least an hour if the two people met face-to-face.

A deadline may dictate the duration of a negotiation – or at least determine when it must be concluded. Provided both people accept that a conclusion must be reached by a specified date, a deadline can be an extremely effective influence in preventing long, inconclusive arguments, and in encouraging a constructive effort to reach agreement.

Joint acceptance of the deadline is important. For one person just to announce that they require a conclusion by a set date may merely cause resentment. There should be some reason for the deadline that both parties understand and accept. There are two ways of approaching this:

- It may be possible to obtain a ruling about a deadline from a senior manager; or circumstances themselves may dictate a date (eg if something is needed for the year-end accounts).

- In the absence of any such externally created deadline, it may be possible to agree a target date. You might say to your colleague, 'I know this problem is an awkward one for both of us, but shall we agree to resolve it by the end of the month?'

Deadlines are therefore useful to concentrate attention on the need to agree outcomes, rather than on extraneous but influential factors such as reputation. The exception is when timing is not critical and when pressing for an early conclusion might result in damaging deadlock. In those cases, you need either to take more time or to defer discussion to a more favourable period.

- Consider whether the issue would best be resolved with a brisk, no-nonsense discussion, or by a lengthier period of negotiation – taking into account the complexity of the issue, the other person's style and probable negotiating position, and your own preferred mode of discussion.

- Use deadlines to encourage a constructive concentration of attention on the need to reach agreement.

Work pressure

Heavy work pressure can have a negative or positive influence on negotiating. The down side is that too little time may be set aside for preparation, or the discussion itself may be conducted too hastily because of impatience to go on to other work. On the other hand the dominance of work objectives may help to concentrate attention on priorities and thus override some of the more peripheral influences that can have an adverse effect on negotiation.

If both parties are equally affected by work pressures, it should be possible to agree how this should influence the timing or content of any discussions eg by saying, 'We're both extremely busy so let's just save time by concentrating on the key point. We can pick up the other issues later.'

It is more difficult if one person is under pressure and the other is not. If you are currently snowed under with a variety of urgent tasks, you will not react kindly to a very relaxed colleague who wants to involve you in a lengthy discussion about matters that, from your viewpoint, have little or no priority. In the reverse situation it would be unwise for you to expect patient co-operation from a work-stressed colleague. In this situation there is little point in persisting in an attempt to obtain such co-operation. The more you press for this, the stronger the negative reaction is likely to be. There are two possible ways of making progress:

- Deal with an issue of some complexity by stages. Pick out just one aspect of an initial short discussion, in the hope that having thus drawn your colleague into at least some involvement, you may be able to make further progress with a series of short meetings.

- Explain that the matter is important and must be given attention, but suggest (tactfully) that your colleague might delegate the discussion to another member of staff eg say, 'I know you are very hard pressed at the moment, so I would be very willing to have discussions with your deputy and just involve you before a decision is finalised.'

If *you* are the person under pressure, you might initiate the suggestion that the matter be delegated, making sure your representative is fully briefed, knows the limits to any necessary concession and reports back to you to clear any final decision. The important point is not to allow work pressure adversely to influence the conduct or outcome of the negotiation.

- Consider whether you or the other person (or both) may be adversely influenced by pressure of work in how you conduct the negotiation and agree its outcome.

- If this is a factor, take corrective action such as dealing only with key issues, or staggering the discussion, or delegating the negotiation.

Location

In many informal situations the choice of whose office is used for a discussion is of little or no relevance. It may be more important in a formal setting, particularly when there may be a choice between meeting on home ground and going outside the organisation, perhaps to negotiate with an important customer. When a choice is possible, in which location would you feel more confident? Even in colleague-to-colleague discussions some people do feel inhibited – sometimes in quite subtle ways – by being in the other person's 'territory'. Are there reasons other than personal confidence in choosing the negotiating location?

There may be practical advantages in the selection of location. Some of the benefits of 'playing at home', in addition to feeling comfortable, are:

- immediate access to information, files etc which may be useful to support or clarify issues arising in the course of the discussion

- immediate access to your own staff in case it becomes helpful to involve any of them in the discussion

- ability to 'set the scene' – eg by having relevant charts on display

- control of seating arrangements, timing of refreshments etc.

There may, however, be advantages in 'playing away':

● Offering to go to the other person's location may be appreciated as a helpful gesture.

■ Particularly with external contacts, you can gain a useful impression of the other person's style and status by seeing where they work.

▲ It is easier to bring the discussion to a close at the optimum moment by explaining your need to leave for an appointment back in your own office.

Other factors to consider are seating arrangements and measures to prevent interruptions. Negotiating from behind a desk creates a less friendly and more formal or status-conscious impression than moving to easy chairs around a coffee table. Uncontrolled interruptions, whether by telephone or people, can seriously affect a discussion of any complexity or sensitivity. It may be helpful, however, to plan a refreshment break, which may be either at a time you announce in advance or left for you to decide at an appropriate moment – perhaps when the discussion shows signs of becoming repetitive or when a break would allow emotions to cool.

● Weigh up the advantages and disadvantages of meeting in your own or the other person's location.

■ If you choose your own location, plan to use this to best effect – by displaying charts, arranging seating and refreshment, and controlling interruptions.

Influence update

At the beginning of this chapter, you were asked some general questions about the extent to which you had been aware of the effect of influence. Now that you have studied this in more detail, answer the following questions and compare your present with your earlier answers:

Type of influence	Have you ever consciously used this factor to support your own case?		Have you ever been adversely affected by other people's use of this factor?	
	Yes	No	Yes	No
Personal relationships				
Status differences				
Connections				
Formality				
Information and expertise				
Gender, race and age				
Reputation				
Expectations				
Timing				
Work pressures				
Location				

3 persuasion

The importance of persuasive skills

Effective negotiators achieve their results partly by understanding the factors that influence people's attitudes and behaviour, and partly by exercising a range of skills that can be described in general terms as persuasion. All managers need to develop these skills, because much of a manager's activity is concerned with resolving issues on which people have different views but need to agree about solutions. The better a manager is at convincing other people of the need to accept or support a particular course of action, the less frequently serious disagreements will get in the way of progress, or decisions have to be imposed by senior management. The effective manager is a persuasive manager. Before looking in detail at persuasive skills, answer the questions in the table on page 36 about any recent occasion when you were involved in a discussion of some complexity, and were trying to persuade a colleague to agree to your view of what should be done, while they began by objecting or arguing for a very different solution.

	Yes	No

- Did either of you get angry at any stage?
- Did you interrupt when the other person made statements you disagreed with?
- Did you do most of the talking?
- Were you surprised when the other person's motivation eventually became evident?
- Did you have to make unplanned concessions to get agreement?
- Were you disconcerted at any time by the other person raising unexpected issues?
- Did you find yourself agreeing to things you were actually unhappy about but could not think quickly how to rebut?
- Did the discussion leave either you or the other person feeling they had lost?
- Would the event be better described as an argument rather than a discussion?
- Did the eventual solution fail to met your original aim?
- Looking back, do you wish you had handled it differently?

If you answered 'yes' to two or more questions (particularly if they included the last two questions) there is probably scope for you to improve your skills of persuasion and negotiation.

There is no single characteristic of persuasiveness: it is an amalgam of skills considered in this chapter under the following headings:

- style – confrontational or collaborative
- the other person's viewpoint
- talking and listening
- probing and questioning
- using adjournments
- concessions and compromise
- summarising
- reaching agreement
- body language.

Style

The quality of any sort of negotiation is determined primarily by the tone set by whoever starts the meeting. There are two extremes – confrontational or collaborative.

Inexperienced negotiators sometimes act as though their virility was under threat, and adopt an abrupt, aggressive stance – though often this stems from fear of having to compromise rather than from the strength of the case they are putting. Occasionally, too, an experienced but manipulative negotiator will adopt this confrontational approach when dealing with someone they recognise as inexperienced or nervous. A common ploy, designed to knock an 'opponent' off-balance, is to open the meeting with a wholly unexpected complaint or demand eg 'I know we are here to talk about unit costs, but I'm not willing to get into this until you explain why you failed to supply me with accurate, quality data yesterday!'

Note the personalised nature of this kind of attack ('I... you... you... me' etc). Whether conscious or not, this personalisation tends to turn the aim of the discussion into a win-or-lose battle between two people rather than an attempt to find a solution to the topic under discussion.

The confrontational approach cannot be recommended, even if it appears to succeed in a few cases. The problem is that such cases generate resentment and undermine any later requirement for the two people concerned to work in collaboration. In any event, the aggressive stance can quickly be punctured, so long as the person targeted stays calm and responds firmly. A response to the attack quoted above might be 'I hear what you say, but that is not what this meeting is for. I'm very willing to discuss quality data, but only after we have settled the unit cost question.'

The most productive style is the collaborative or problem-solving approach. This sets aside any personal feelings about winning or losing and concentrates on the issue to be resolved. In this approach the fact that the other person holds a different view or seeks a different outcome is not seen as a personal challenge. It simply creates a situation both parties need to resolve. In essence your message to the other person is 'We have a problem that we have to discuss in order to find a solution that satisfies both of us' – and not 'If it wasn't for you there wouldn't be a problem, so I want you to back off and accept my solution!'

This does not mean that you should have no targeted outcome – simply that the most effective way to work towards your goal is for the solution to emerge as a jointly agreed solution. This is often described in the literature on negotiation as a 'win/win' approach. You begin by establishing rapport with the other person, go on to explore different views and alternatives without rancour, and conclude with an agreement for which both parties feel a sense of ownership and satisfaction.

This may sound idealistic, but it does not imply an absence of vigorous debate or any need weakly to abandon important points of principle or priority. We are considering style, not content. This style recognises that a conflict of ideas (as distinct from a conflict between individuals) is often constructive because it means that all the angles are tested in discussion and debate. The persuasive negotiator has determination, but it is determination to find a solution or reach agreement, not determination to secure a personal victory. *Set a tone for the whole discussion that concentrates attention on the need to reach an agreed conclusion by joint problem-solving.*

The other person's viewpoint

One of the most important factors in developing persuasive skills is to discipline yourself continually to look at your objectives (and how you are trying to achieve them) from the other person's viewpoint. You cannot order them to agree with you, and yet you require their involvement – but why should they be co-operative? Putting it crudely, what's in it for them?

You certainly cannot rely on other people adopting a wholly altruistic attitude and agreeing with you simply to be helpful. If your colleagues sometimes behave this way, that is a bonus – yet not something it is realistic to expect on every occasion. Most people are concerned most of the time with how their agreement to any request might benefit them, not you. The fact that you have a problem is, by definition, your problem, not theirs – unless you can show them:

- *either* that if they fail to address the issue constructively they will probably experience a problem themselves

- *or* that if they help you find a solution they may gain some benefit.

The more you can stress benefits, the more readily you will be able to persuade. In sales training this is described as selling 'sunny-side up'. It means you need to think how any proposal you are putting forward will be seen by the other person. They will be considering what the effects of conceding to your request will be to them. Will it cause them any difficulties? Or might there be some advantage – even if this is only the avoidance of possible trouble later?

To give an example: you approach your organisation's research officer because you need an up-to-date market share analysis for a marketing report for the Board. You need the analysis very quickly, but you know the research officer is extremely busy with other high-priority work. Here are three different approaches. Which do you think would be the most effective?

1. 'I have an urgent need for a market share analysis, updated to the end of last week, and I must have it by Friday midday at the latest.'

2. 'I have to include a market share analysis updated to the end of last week for an important Board report, and I need it by Friday midday. I know you're busy, but I'm afraid that if I have to use older figures I will need to explain to the Board that you were unable to supply updated figures.'

3. 'I would like to use an updated market analysis to illustrate a major point in a report the Board have asked for urgently. If you were possibly able to produce the figures by, say, lunchtime on Friday, I would be very happy to give your assistance a specific mention in the report.'

You probably (and correctly) selected no. 3. The response to the first approach, which does not even explain why the analysis is needed, would probably be 'Sorry, I've got too much other work.' The second approach might be successful, but its use of a threat would probably generate resentment, and the analysis would be done reluctantly. The third approach offers a benefit – a personal mention in a Board report – and would therefore be more likely to generate a helpful response. Even then it might prove necessary to agree to some change in your preferred outcome – such as a simplification of the analysis you had originally intended – in order to achieve full agreement. But the principle is the same: finding ways of offering the other person a beneficial reason for them to be co-operative. Concessions of this kind are discussed in more detail later in this chapter, but the key points are:

- Consider the matter under discussion from the other person's viewpoint. Try to identify and 'sell' to them the benefits that would result from their accepting your case.

- Be prepared to alter your position (within acceptable limits) in order to achieve this approach.

Talking and listening

The two components of any discussion are talking and listening. Saying the right things in the right way at the right time, knowing when not to speak, and listening extremely carefully to what the other person says, are the essential characteristics of the skilled persuader.

Inexperienced negotiators often feel under a compulsion not just to initiate the discussion but also to set out their whole case as quickly and comprehensively as possible. One symptom of a lack of confidence is compulsive talking – which includes the frequent interruption of the other person whenever they say something with which the negotiator disagrees. This carries three risks:

● You give your whole argument away too early, leaving no space quietly to change the way you put your case in the light of the other person's arguments.

■ If you do not allow the other person to complete what they have to say, you may not hear things you need to know in order to understand how they are thinking.

▲ By continual interruption you will cause irritation rather than encourage co-operation.

The wise approach is to develop a dialogue with the other person, giving them every opportunity to say what they wish to, and build up your case as the discussion proceeds. The starting-point can be along these lines: 'The general point we need to discuss is x, which has occurred because of y. But before I go into any detail it would be helpful if you outlined your general view.'

A great deal of restraint can be needed to stop oneself interrupting when the other person makes a confusing or incorrect statement. It is best, however, to allow them to finish before responding, and then to avoid terminology that implies personal criticism. So instead of interrupting to say, 'You are wrong about that', wait for them to finish and say something like, 'Could you explain a bit more about z because it doesn't quite line up with my understanding of that point.'

Attentive listening is essential if you are to discover the way the other person's mind is working. For example, people are often very sensitive or cautious about making concessions, and the first sign that they may be thinking of changing their position may be, ironically, statements such as:

- 'There is no possibility of my agreeing at this stage.'

- 'I can't accept your proposals in their current form.'

The *real* messages that the good listener will deduce from these apparently negative statements may be:

- 'Give me a little more time and I might be able to agree.'

- 'If you repackage your proposals I would find it easier to accept them.'

It is also important to listen not just to the words but to how they are said. Are statements being made confidently, or with some hesitation? Are there signs of irritation or impatience?

Is there an immediate rejection of your proposals, or can you detect some willingness to consider them? These are the types of question you should be asking yourself while the discussion proceeds. Listening is as important as talking.

● Do not state the whole of your case at the beginning: encourage a dialogue with the other person and develop your case as the discussion proceeds.

■ Do not interrupt when the other person makes statements that you disagree with or that are incorrect: wait for them to finish and then use impersonal terminology to achieve corrections, rather than making personal criticisms.

▲ Be an attentive listener to the tone, as well as the substance, of what is said.

Probing and questioning

Just as you are trying to persuade the other person in a negotiation to accept your views or proposals, so they will try to persuade you. If they can show that the ideas they put forward achieve better results than your solution, it is not a matter of weakness to be persuaded. What is important, however, is that their case should be very thoroughly examined – largely through probing questions – so that you can be confident of making a sound assessment of its strengths and weaknesses.

There are three common flaws in the way negotiators argue their cases:

- making factually incorrect statements
- omitting relevant factual information
- misusing statistics.

Each should be looked for and tested, if necessary, by your asking questions. Questioning is generally much more effective than simply making statements asserting the other person is wrong.

In a discussion, for example, about proposed changes to delivery dates one person may make a statement such as 'You've missed the dates on 10 per cent of the deliveries over the past 12 months.' If this is a significant point, it should not be allowed to stand without proof. So the question in response might be 'Can you show me the relevant delivery schedules?' These may reveal a less serious situation, the person making the statement having succumbed to the temptation to exaggerate in order to make a point.

An even more common fault is to argue on factual grounds but omit facts that, although relevant, happen not to support one's case. The 10 per cent delivery failure may be an accurate figure, but is misleading because no mention is made of a lengthy rail dispute during the period concerned. A calmly placed question such as 'How many of those deliveries were affected by the rail dispute?' can be much more effective than a belligerent 'You are conveniently forgetting the rail strike!'

It is equally important to be wary of accepting the validity of certain statistics – particularly averages and percentages when very small numbers of cases are involved. Thus, in a negotiation about office rentals one person may state that the average new rental for the area is £100 per square metre. An appropriate probing question would be 'How many new rentals are included in that figure, and what were the lowest and highest rentals?' This may reveal that the average is almost meaningless, as only six cases were involved and the figure was distorted by one very high rental for an unusual prestige building.

In addition to these three specific flaws there are often parts of a discussion when the other person makes statements that are faulty in logic or seem contradictory. Again, rather than challenging these by counter-statements (eg 'You're wrong!'), it is better to probe by putting further questions such as:

● 'Can you explain your thinking about that more fully?'

■ 'I haven't fully grasped the logic of that: could you put it a different way?'

▲ 'Could you explain the connection between that point and the one you made earlier about x?'

Faced with questions of this kind, the other person may realise for themselves that their argument is flawed – rather than having you tell them so. Exposing flaws tactfully is a powerfully persuasive tool. *Probe the other person's case with shrewd and tactful questioning for flaws of fact and logic.*

Using adjournments

Experienced negotiators frequently make effective use of breaks or adjournments in a discussion. These may not be relevant to short, informal discussions, but the principles are worth noting for possible application to any negotiating situation. Adjournments can be used for two main purposes:

● to give those concerned an opportunity to consider new points or proposals before making any commitments

■ to bring a halt to a discussion that has become too emotionally charged.

Inexperienced negotiators can be overinfluenced by pressure from the other person to agree quickly to proposals to which they have as yet given inadequate attention. It is important to resist this pressure, and one way of doing so is to be quite open about your need for time to think. Just say, 'That's an interesting idea but I need a little time to consider it. Let's have a break, and resume in half an hour.'

Discussions do sometimes become heated, and good solutions are rarely possible when tempers are raised. It is remarkable how even a very short break at such a time can result in a greatly improved atmosphere when the discussion resumes. It just needs someone to take the initiative and say something like 'We seem to be getting bogged down. I think it might be a good idea if we have a quick break for a cup of tea at this point and resume in 10 minutes.' *Use adjournments to gain time to consider new points and to break situations in which relationships have become strained.*

Concessions and compromise

The best outcome of a discussion may appear to be when you persuade the other person to accept your unaltered proposal or point of view – but this is not necessarily either possible or desirable. The other person's input to the discussion may reveal factors that you have failed to take into account but that should influence the outcome. Their commitment to implementing a solution will be improved by a sense of involvement. It may simply be impossible to make progress without making some concessions.

This element of negotiation involves general attitudes as well as specific skills of persuasion. Attitudinally, you need to focus on the issue under discussion and remain determined to reach an agreed outcome – rather than determined to hold to your original decision or to beat your opponent. The skills are concerned partly with timing, and partly with the way possible concessions or compromises are introduced into the discussion.

There comes a point in most discussions when both people have fully explained their respective opening positions and a danger arises of these arguments' simply being repeated. When this happens, the tendency is for views to harden, as more and more reasons are thought of why compromise is unacceptable. This point needs to be recognised and the discussion moved on to a more exploratory and constructive phase. You might say, for example, 'It might be helpful, now we both understand each other's views, to spend some time looking at possible ways forward.'

It is generally a mistake, however, to jump straight to putting clear-cut proposals. People need time to think about possible changes to their position and often react badly to any apparent attempt to rush them into a decision. You need also to be wary of offering some concession without making clear that you expect something in return. The technique is to float ideas without commitment on either side. Typical ways of generating discussion are:

- 'As a matter of interest, what might your views be if I suggested x?'

- 'Suppose we did something along these lines, what might be your response?'

- 'I wondered if you had given any thought to x? If you could do this, I might be able to do something about y.'

- 'Would it help you to agree to x if I was able to defer taking action on y?'

A key point to remember when discussing concessions and compromise is the importance of encouraging the other person to feel positive about changing their position – ie not making them feel they are losing. A change may be of great benefit to you, but that is not the point to emphasise. You need to help the other person recognise the personal benefits of any compromise they might agree to. So applaud their helpfulness and wisdom – don't gloat about getting your own way. You may well float an idea they eventually agree to, but when they do, the thing to say is something like 'I really appreciate that. It's an ingenious idea and I'm very grateful to you for thinking of such a good solution.'

● Do not allow a discussion to go on too long without tactfully moving on to talk about the concessions or compromises that may be necessary to achieve an agreed outcome.

■ Introduce possible concessions and compromises by floating ideas on a no-commitment basis.

▲ Ensure possible concessions on your part are seen as linked to moves by the other person.

Summarising

There are two quite serious risks in lengthy and complex discussions:

● Points agreed verbally at different stages of the discussion may be remembered differently by the two parties by the time the negotiation is completed. This can then lead to a secondary dispute about what has or has not been agreed.

■ At the final stage of agreement, a manipulative negotiator may try to reopen discussion on items agreed verbally at an earlier stage in order to squeeze out some last-minute concessions.

These risks can be avoided by pausing in the discussion at appropriate moments, taking stock of where it has reached, and confirming with a written note anything agreed so far. This can be initiated by a suggestion such as 'I would now find it helpful if we could just summarise where we have reached. If we also make a note of what we have agreed so far it will help us to avoid going over ground later that we have already covered. As I understand it, we have dealt with *a*, *b* and *c*, and agreed *x*, *y* and *z*. If you're happy with that I'll make a brief note and we can then move on to *d*, *e* and *f*.' *In lengthy or complex discussions, use summaries to prevent later disagreement about what has or has not been discussed and agreed.*

Reaching agreement

After a period in which various options have been considered it can be quite difficult to bring a discussion to a firm and mutually satisfactory conclusion. But there comes a point when ideas and possibilities for a solution can no longer be discussed hypothetically or on a no-commitment basis:

someone has to take the initiative and put forward a clearly defined proposal.

Timing is again important. Most discussions have highs and lows, and the time to conclude an agreement is obviously when there is a collaborative, not confrontational, atmosphere. In a lengthy negotiation this might well be after an adjournment agreed for the specific purpose of allowing both parties to consider their final positions in the light of all the previous discussion. Otherwise it is a matter of judgement as to when the other person will be most receptive to a proposed solution.

As with the floating of possible solutions, so the persuasive approach to making a final proposal is to emphasise its benefits to the other person. In addition it is necessary to be very firm about the finality of a proposal that genuinely represents the limit to any compromise. Inexperienced negotiators often weaken their ability to take this stance because they have described earlier positions as final, only to agree to further compromise. 'Final' must mean 'final'. This is best emphasised by explaining why no further concessions can be made and perhaps by pointing out the consequences that might flow from deadlock, such as having to refer the matter to a senior manager, or (in the event of formal negotiations) to external arbitration.

After a difficult discussion, particularly if it has lasted far longer than was originally intended, there is a temptation to agree to almost any solution that seems to offer a quick settlement. There are three common dangers in this:

● Some key points, such as implementation dates, may be overlooked causing problems when the agreement comes to be implemented. A good question to ask after something has been agreed in principle is 'Who is going to do what, by when, in order to put this agreement into effect?'

■ Unless what has been agreed is immediately summarised and noted, the two persons may leave the discussion with different interpretations of what their agreement really means. The final summary is a vital part of any negotiation.

▲ The agreement may be 'fudged', simply to avoid any further argument. You ask a colleague to provide you with certain information earlier than he or she is initially willing to. After a long discussion they say, 'OK, I'll do what I can to bring the date forward.' What does this mean? It might result in no more than a frustrating wait for information that still arrives too late. You should either continue to press for a specific, latest acceptable date or perhaps say, 'Can you come back to me tomorrow with a firm date after you have had time to assess what you can do?'

Reaching a mutually satisfactory conclusion is the primary objective of any negotiation, and more care needs to be taken at this final point than at any stage in the discussion.

● Exercise judgement in picking the best time to bring the discussion to a conclusion.

■ If you make a final proposal, be sure it *is* final, and explain why.

▲ Ensure the final agreement includes all necessary points, is clearly understood, and is not expressed in ambiguous terms.

Body language

All the preceding headings in this chapter have dealt with verbal interaction. But the quality of communication between two people in a discussion is also influenced or made evident by body language. In verbal communication attentive and perceptive listening provides valuable clues about the other person's attitude. Observation of their posture, the way they sit and gesticulate, can provide further clues. For example, you make a statement and the other person sits back and folds their arms. This is probably a sign that they are unimpressed, or even offended. Leaning forward generally indicates interest. Face-touching is often connected with doubt or puzzlement. Eyebrow-raising is a classic indication of surprise.

Most indications of this kind are unconscious, but some gestures can be used intentionally. For example, one way of indicating that the exploratory part of a discussion is at an end is to gather up one's papers or to close an open file. When stating something like 'After taking everything into account, our final position is x', the finality of this statement can be reinforced by a firm hand-gesture – placing it palm-down on the table.

The interpretation of body language needs to be used with caution – it is not an exact science. But to overlook the signals that can be read from posture, gesture and facial expression is to miss a potentially rich source of indications of attitudes and intentions. *Observe the other person's body language for clues about their reactions and attitude, and use gesture to reinforce your own message.*

How effective are you as a persuader?

Now you have worked through this chapter on persuasion, assess your own skills by answering the questionnaire below, and compare the results with those for the questionnaire at the beginning of the chapter.

	Rate yourself on a scale of 1 to 5			
	Rarely			Always
	1	2	3	4	5

1. I adopt a positive and collaborative style.
2. I am successful in avoiding confrontation.
3. I assess the other person's viewpoint.

(continued opposite)

4. I adapt my position to reflect the other person's viewpoint.

5. I encourage a dialogue, and do not set out all my case immediately.

6. I do not interrupt the other person when they make statements I disagree with.

7. I am a very attentive listener.

8. I use questions, not statements, to probe or challenge the other person's case.

9. If I need time for thought, or for emotions to cool, I seek an adjournment.

10. I first introduce proposals for compromise or concession on a no-commitment basis.

11. I link my proposed concessions to moves by the other person.

12. I emphasise the benefits to the other person of proposed compromise.

13. I use summaries to ensure mutual understanding and move the discussion on.

14. I take the initiative in bringing the discussion to a constructive close.

15. I ensure any agreement includes details of how it will be implemented.

16. I ensure any agreement is mutually understood and is not ambiguous.

17. I observe body language for clues about attitudes and intentions.

stages in the discussion process

Discussions that progress effectively from initial differences to eventual agreed conclusions normally follow the same general sequence, even though in informal situations this may not be immediately evident. Some aspects have been mentioned earlier, such as the transition from an exchange of views to an exploration of possible solutions. It is helpful, however, to set out the full sequence so that this can be used as a check-list for your own negotiating episodes. The stages are:

- ● preparation
- ■ exchanging initial views
- ▲ exploring possible compromise
- ◉ searching for common ground
- ◍ securing agreement
- ● implementing the agreement.

The first and last of these stages take place before and after the actual discussion, and there may be a view that they are not part of the actual process of influencing and persuading. This would be short-sighted. Without adequate preparation the full effects of relevant influences are unlikely to be utilised or recognised. And unless thought is given within the discussion to how any agreement is to be implemented, the benefits of an agreement may not be realised.

Preparation

Before entering any kind of negotiation, you should be confident on two counts:

- that you are fully briefed on the subject matter and are unlikely to be caught out by the other person's introducing unexpected facts or figures

- that you are clear about what you want to achieve.

Your confidence can be badly shaken if, in the course of a discussion, the other person is able to show that information or data you are using to support your case are inaccurate or incomplete. Time spent on research or acquiring expert advice is often time saved and results achieved within the discussion itself.

In considering objectives, it is necessary to be realistic about the chances of persuading the other person to accept your ideal solution, and to be prepared to lower your expectations if the ideal cannot be achieved. The important point is then to be very clear (and very firm) about your 'bottom line' – the lowest acceptable outcome. Aim to do better than this, but know your sticking-point.

In the preparation stage you need also to think how best to argue your case, paying particular attention to the other person's likely viewpoint and objectives. Before starting a discussion:

● Be sure you know enough about the subject matter.

■ Decide your objectives and bottom line.

▲ Decide how best to put your case.

Exchanging initial views

In the discussion itself it is unwise to plunge straight into requests or proposals, or to start arguing the pros and cons of each person's position. It is better to spend a little time simply setting out and explaining the starting positions. Understanding what the other person's problem is and why their view differs from yours is of great assistance when it comes to developing possible solutions later.

In this initial stage it is consequently helpful to encourage the other person to say as much as possible, rather than be tempted immediately to challenge anything they say which you know to be incorrect or feel to be illogical. The more they say, the better you will understand them. The better you understand them, the easier it should be to find solutions they will feel able to accept. *Allow time at the beginning of a discussion for a straightforward exchange and explanation of views, and encourage the other person to talk fully about their problems and perceptions.*

Exploring possible compromise

The need to move on from an exchange of views to the exploration of possible solutions was considered in Chapter 3. That chapter also explained the value of floating ideas on a no-commitment basis and of emphasising the benefits to the other person of any concession or compromise.

In this stage it is not uncommon to find one person putting forward all the constructive ideas and the other person simply responding negatively. You need to encourage the other person to come up with ideas of their own, not merely to react. A response to a negative comment can be 'I understand your difficulty with that, but what alternative do you think we might consider?' As with so many aspects of negotiation, questions are often more effective than statements. *Try not to be the one making all the suggestions. By asking questions and by avoiding a negative approach yourself, encourage the other person to contribute constructively to the exploration of ideas and possible solutions.*

Searching for common ground

There is a tendency to concentrate on those aspects in a discussion where there are differences of view. Two inexperienced negotiators can spend a long time disagreeing with each other, and the result can too easily be a bad-tempered argument.

If the objective of achieving an agreed solution is kept firmly in mind, it will become evident that the most productive approach is to build on those aspects on which both parties can agree. In other words, move from a cautious, no-commitment exploration of possibilities to a purposeful search for common ground. This is often helped by setting the discussion in its broader context and by referring to some of the influences described in Chapter 3. There may be disagreement on points of detail, but both parties may share the same interest in, for example,

- promoting the organisation's core values
- contributing to organisational success
- avoiding extra costs or waste
- achieving a quick solution so other work can be attended to
- wanting to be recognised as a helpful problem-solver
- wanting to foster good working relationships.

Thus the colleague who is reluctant to provide you with market data might be encouraged towards being more helpful by emphasising the value to the Board of the information you require – the common ground being a wish by both parties to contribute to important Board discussions. And if the colleague indicates that he or she might possibly do something to help (however minor), it is this willingness that should be built on – not the fact that at this stage he or she has still not fully agreed to your request. *In the latter stage of a discussion, concentrate and build on those matters on which you and the other person agree.*

Securing agreement

Most aspects of this final stage have already been considered under the heading of 'reaching agreement' (see page 52). It is worth re-emphasising, however, that the whole purpose of the discussion is to achieve a mutually satisfactory outcome, and that there are risks at this point of an otherwise constructive discussion failing at the last moment to deliver a sound agreement. Two common reasons for such failure are:

- reluctance to agree to a sensible compromise solution because of the loss of face in so doing. If you detect this as a personal tendency, remind yourself of the impersonal or work-related primary objective and try to set personal feelings aside. If you detect this as a factor in the other person's attitude, do all you can to make it easy for them to agree eg by showing gratitude and pointing to the benefits to them and the organisation of resolving the matter.

- the last-minute introduction, by a manipulative or reluctant negotiator, of a completely new condition as a bargaining chip to secure agreement.

This new condition may be a peripheral point that has not figured in the previous discussion, or even something wholly unconnected with the matter under discussion. Your colleague might say, 'OK, I'll produce the data you need by the month end if you can agree to let me have the extra office space we talked about last week' (referring to a wholly unrelated issue). While it may occasionally be acceptable to agree to such a proposal, it is generally unwise to accede to this type of pressure. It solves one problem – but only at the expense of another. You may also acquire a reputation as someone easy to manipulate. In most cases it is best to call the other person's bluff and pleasantly, but firmly, refuse. They have, after all, conceded the practicability of the solution you are seeking.

It is acceptable, however, to use a final small concession on a matter involved in the issue under discussion to clinch an agreement. For instance, you have almost persuaded your colleague to accept a Thursday deadline for the information you need, but he or she still holds back from saying OK. So at the last minute you say you could cope if data on one item was not available until Friday. You will probably find you receive all the data on Thursday, because the concession you agreed was more important to the person as a symbol they had not conceded everything, rather than as a genuinely relevant work issue.

● Recognise and avoid the risk of a last-minute failure to agree, which can result from fear of losing face by accepting a compromise.

■   Do not allow peripheral or unrelated issues to be used as last-minute bargaining chips.

▲   Use relevant but minor concessions to overcome last-minute reluctance to agree.

Implementing the agreement

Agreements are not effective until they have been implemented. On simple topics the measures to secure implementation may be obvious, but there is sometimes a need to agree a specific implementation action plan. Sometimes agreements even fall apart because, although there is consensus about principles and objectives, the parties concerned cannot agree the detailed process needed to put these into effect. The implementation points that may need to be considered are:

●   a schedule of action points for what has to be done

■   deadlines for each action point

▲   agreement on who will take the lead on each action point

●   a schedule of any additional resources or information that may be needed

●   a schedule of who needs to be informed and/or involved, in addition to the persons who have made the agreement

●   how action is to be monitored and co-ordinated

■   how the effectiveness of the agreement is to be assessed.

The approach to adopt is this: a discussion has not really been concluded until the solution reached has been successfully implemented. *Ensure that any agreement includes a clear understanding or action plan for the measures needed to secure its successful implementation.*

further study

Reading

FOWLER A. *Negotiation: Skills and strategies.* London, IPM, 1990.

The companion text to this Management Shapers publication, *Negotiation* deals at greater length with the same topics, with particular emphasis on the skills needed in intermanagerial relationships and in formal negotiations. The text includes numerous case-studies illustrating how the principles of influence and persuasion are applicable to a wide range of organisational and managerial situations.

GILLEN T. *Positive Influencing Skills.* London, IPD, 1995.

Leading trainer and consultant Terry Gillen offers practical, in-depth advice on getting people onto your own wavelength in a wide range of situations: coaching, counselling, criticising, disciplining, and negotiating.

HONEY P. *Improve Your People Skills.* 2nd edn. London, IPD, 1997.

The skills involved in working effectively with others are explored by the author: how your behaviour influences the perceptions and behaviour of those around you.

LAMBERT T. *The Power of Influence.* London, Nicholas Brealey Publishing, 1995.

Tom Lambert outlines the skills needed for influencing employees, colleagues, and customers in a business setting.

SARGENT A. *Turning People On: The motivation challenge.* London, IPM, 1990.

Andrew Sargent explains how to gain the commitment of the workforce through the use of motivation skills, including influencing and persuasion skills.

Training videos

BBC TRAINING VIDEOS. *It's a Deal.*

Describes the win/win approach to negotiation.

CONNAUGHT TRAINING SERVICES. *It's a Deal!*

A widely used video about negotiation, including the skills necessary for influence and persuasion. (Also available from Melrose and from Gower.)

MELROSE FILM PRODUCTIONS LTD. *Agreed.*

How to achieve co-operation and agreement from people who are, initially, uncooperative.

Other titles in the *Management Shapers* series:

The Appraisal Discussion

Terry Gillen

The Appraisal Discussion shows you how to make appraisal a productive and motivating experience for all levels of performer – and help your credibility in the process! Practical advice is given on:

- assessing performance fairly and accurately

- using feedback, including constructive criticism and targeted praise, to improve performance

- handling 'difficult' appraisees

- encouraging and supporting reluctant appraisees

- setting, and gaining commitment to, worthwhile objectives

- avoiding common appraiser problems from inadvertent bias to 'appraisal speak'

- identifying ways to develop appraisees so they add value to the organisation.

First Edition
96 pages
Pbk
0 85292 751 7
1998
£5.95

Asking Questions

Ian MacKay

Asking Questions will help you ask the 'right' questions, using the correct form to elicit a useful response. All managers need to hone their questioning skills, whether interviewing, appraising or simply exchanging ideas. This book offers guidance and helpful advice on:

- using various forms of open questions – including probing, simple interrogative, opinion-seeking, hypothetical, extension and precision etc.

- encouraging and drawing out speakers through supportive statements and interjections

- establishing specific facts through closed or 'direct' approaches

- avoiding counter-productive questions

- using questions in a training context.

Second Edition
96 pages
Pbk
0 85292 768 1
November 1998
£5.95

Assertiveness

Terry Gillen

Assertiveness will help you feel naturally confident, enjoy the respect of others and easily establish productive working relationships, even with 'awkward' people. It covers:

- understanding why you behave as you do and, when that behaviour is counter-productive, knowing what to do about it

- understanding other people better

- keeping your emotions under control

- preventing others bullying, flattering or manipulating you against your will

- acquiring easy-to-learn techniques that you can use immediately

- developing your personal assertiveness strategy.

First Edition
96 pages
Pbk
0 85292 769 X
November 1998
£5.95

Constructive Feedback

Roland and Frances Bee

Constructive Feedback plays a vital role in enhancing performance and relationships. The authors help you identify when to give feedback, how best to give it, and how to receive and use feedback yourself. They offer sound, practical advice on:

- distinguishing between 'destructive' criticism and 'constructive' feedback

- using feedback to manage better – as an essential element of coaching, counselling, training and motivating your team

- improving your skills by following the 10 Tools of Giving Constructive Feedback

- dealing with challenging situations and people

- eliciting the right feedback to highlight your strengths and opportunities for your own development.

First Edition
96 pages
Pbk
0 85292 752 5
1998
£5.95

The Disciplinary Interview

Alan Fowler

The Disciplinary Interview will ensure you adopt the correct procedures, conduct productive interviews and manage the outcome with confidence. It offers step-by-step guidance on the whole process, including:

- understanding the legal implications

- investigating the facts

- presenting the management case

- probing the employee's case

- diffusing conflict through skilful listening and questioning

- distinguishing between conduct and competence

- weighing up the alternatives – dismissing or dropping the case; disciplining and improving performance through counselling and training.

First Edition
96 pages
Pbk
0 85292 753 3
1998
£5.95

Leadership Skills

John Adair

Leadership Skills will give you confidence, guide and inspire you on your journey from being an effective manager to becoming a leader of excellence. Acknowledged as a world authority on leadership, Adair offers stimulating insights on:

- recognising and developing your leadership qualities

- acquiring the personal authority to give positive direction and the flexibility to embrace change

- acting on the key interacting needs – to achieve your task, build your team and develop its members

- transforming the core leadership functions such as planning, communicating and motivating, into practical skills you can master.

First Edition
96 pages
Pbk
0 85292 764 9
November 1998
£5.95

Listening Skills

Ian MacKay

Listening Skills describes techniques and activities to improve your ability and makes clear why effective listening is such a crucial management skill – and yet so often overlooked or neglected. Clear explanations will help you:

- recognise the inhibitors to listening

- improve your physical attention so you are seen to be listening

- listen to what is really being said by analysing and evaluating the message

- ask the right questions so you understand what is not being said

- interpret tone of voice and non-verbal signals.

Second Edition
96 pages
Pbk
0 85292 754 1
1998
£5.95

Making Meetings Work

Patrick Forsyth

Making Meeting Work will maximise your time – both before and during meetings – clarify your aims, improve your own and others' performance and make the whole process rewarding and productive – never frustrating and futile. The book is full of practical tips and advice on:

- drawing up objectives and setting realistic agendas

- deciding the who, where and when to meet

- chairing effectively – encouraging discussion, creativity and sound decision-making

- sharpening your skills of observation, listening and questioning to get across your points

- dealing with problem participants

- handling the follow-up – turning decisions into action.

First Edition
96 pages
Pbk
0 85292 765 7
November 1998
£5.95

Motivating People

Iain Maitland

Motivating People will help you maximise individual and team skills to achieve personal, departmental and, above all, organisational goals. It provides practical insights on:

● becoming a better leader and co-ordinating winning teams

▪ identifying, setting and communicating achievable targets

▲ empowering others through simple job improvement techniques

● encouraging self-development, defining training needs and providing helpful assessment

● ensuring pay and workplace conditions make a positive contribution to satisfaction and commitment.

First Edition
96 pages
Pbk
0 85292 766 5
November 1998
£5.95

The Selection Interview

Penny Hackett

The Selection Interview will ensure you choose better people – more efficiently. It provides step-by-step guidance on techniques and procedures from the initial decision to recruit through to the critical final choice. Helpful advice is included on:

- drawing up job descriptions, employee specifications and assessment plans

- setting up the interview

- using different interview strategies and styles

- improving your questioning and listening skills

- evaluating the evidence to reach the best decision.

First Edition
96 pages
Pbk
0 85292 756 8
1998
£5.95

Working in Teams

Alison Hardingham

Working in Teams looks at teamworking from the inside. It will give you invaluable insights into how you can make a more positive and effective contribution – as team member or team leader – to ensure your team works together and achieves together. Clear and practical guidelines are given on:

- understanding the nature and make-up of teams

- finding out if your team is on track

- overcoming the most common teamworking problems

- recognising your own strengths and weaknesses as a team member

- giving teams the tools, techniques and organisational support they need.

First Edition
96 pages
Pbk
0 85292 767 3
November 1998
£5.95